The Stay At Home Tycoon

Copyright © 2012 by Jonathon Brooks

I0473128

Contents

Preface

There are countless books and articles in print and online today that state they can make you money, often quickly and without much effort. This is not one of those books.

What I set out to do with this book is not to entice or dazzle you with promises of wealth or guarantees of success, but rather inform you and bring to your attention the tools and methods available to you if you ever thought to make money online.

You've probably seen ads and information in various forms of media promising to make you money in only a short time. If you have tried some of these methods, I don't have to tell you that the claims are often exaggerated at best and just plain exploitative and laughable at worst. I've compiled a popular list of ideas and techniques people are using today to make extra money, and I promise there are no catches.

Before we begin the first chapter I would like to stress a sentiment and motif you will likely notice throughout the course of this eBook: **making money online requires work; the more you work, the more you make**. I know that such a sentiment is hardly ideal, but it's true. But as long as you view these methods with that thought in mind, I am confident that you can bring in a reasonable amount of income each month. I feel confident in saying because in researching this book, thousands of people were already making money from the methods expressed in the following chapters.

It is my hope that one or more of these chapters will resonate with you in a way that will allow you to create for yourself a whole new way of generating income. We all want to be our own boss when it comes to work, and maybe now you can be.

Chapter 1 – Virtual Assistant

If you're like many people, there stands a good chance that you have never heard of a virtual assistant. Truth is, it's not that much different from an administrative assistant except that the majority of the tasks that are asked of you can be done from the convenience of your home.

Becoming a virtual assistant is ideal for individuals who worked (or currently work) in the corporate world. I say this because many of the tasks asked of you as a virtual assistant are similar to a real desk job. The major difference (and in my opinion, bonus) is that you don't have to worry about a hectic commute or an uncomfortable dress code.

A virtual assistant is exactly what it sounds like; you assist someone virtually. Such tasks might include sending out emails, researching key information, and collecting website traffic stats, to name a few. It really depends on who you are working for and what product or service they are providing or plan on providing. My advice: while keeping your options open, if you are contacted for a virtual assistant position, have a list of questions relating to your expected duties.

There are several sites available where you can get started as a virtual assistant. Many of these sites will let you review the positions available and then bid on them (bidding in this instance means you get to "bid" how much money you would like to be paid for the job). Prospective employers will then read through your qualifications and select someone. I won't say that it won't be competitive at first, but the more good work you do and rapport you build with each client, the better your chances are of landing more jobs with more clients or perhaps something more sustainable with just a few. Some sites you will want to check out for more information on finding work as a virtual assistant include Odesk, Freelancer, Elance, and Guru (a simple

Google search will reveal these sites for you).

Food for Thought
Stay up to date. No prospective employer wants to look at an outdated resume or portfolio. If you can, constantly try to gather new skills and experience that might elevate you above others who vie for the same position.

If you are a newcomer to the world of virtual assistance, I would recommend that you join all of these sites and any other legitimate ones you can find. At first it can very much be a numbers game. You'll want to answer as many ads and bid for as many jobs until you finally land a few. Once you do land some though you'll find that people who need to hire a virtual assistant will be hesitant to let a good one go. So do your best job and hopefully you'll start working with only those regular clients you enjoy.

Of all the online moneymaking ideas in this book this is perhaps the simplest one. You basically sign up for sites, and look for people who need virtual assistants. You then try to excel at all the tasks given to you to build long-term relationships with these clients.

A Quick Review...

Alright, so let's review quickly the things you will need to keep in mind (and do) when beginning your path as a virtual assistant:

- ❖ Get your resume or portfolio up to date and ready
- ❖ Find one or more websites catering to prospective virtual assistants (i.e. Odesk, Freelancer, Elance, Guru, etc.)
- ❖ Respond to as many ads as you can. Work on building your skill set and rapport with various employers. With

luck you can find something on a more permanent basis.

The rest will be up to your ability to coordinate effectively with potential employers, the solidity/quality of your work, and the strength of your work ethic.

Chapter 2 – eBay

Most everyone in today's modern world is familiar with the online auction site, eBay. The function of the site is relatively simple. Buyers search eBay for an item they might find themselves wanting, and if it's available they can place a bid. The highest bid by the end of the auction wins the item. In some cases, there is a "Buy Now" button to completely bypass the auction process and instantly purchase the item (although the instant purchase price is often higher than the auction price at its end).

So how can you make money with eBay? While you may think to sell some old collectibles and antiques you have lying around in the attic or storage, getting rid of these items will not provide a sustainable cash flow. Instead of seeing eBay as an auction hall of the digital world, try instead to envision it as a global bazaar; a place where many vendors can distribute their wares to a large customer base.

To make money on eBay, you simply have to embrace the foundation of capitalism. You do this by buying stock goods and reselling them for a profit. It's the exact same process that all those stores you go to run on, except YOU'RE the one incorporating it and you're doing it from home. Profit is generated by buying stock immediately from retailers or wholesalers and then listing items on eBay for sale. When someone buys one of your items, you collect their payment and then complete the transaction by sending their purchase on its way. If you don't have a lot of starting capital or don't want to mess around with the potential headaches shipping can inspire, then you may want to utilize the services of a drop shipper.

Drop shippers are companies that will deliver an item for you. The benefits of using a drop shipper are that you won't actually pay for an item until a customer orders it from you, and you won't have to physically receive/ ship the item yourself. Some drop shippers will charge a fee to start doing business with them, but many will only charge the price of the item you are buying. For example, an item may be $8.99, but you may have it listed at $10.99 on eBay. When a customer orders you collect their $10.99, pay $8.99 to the drop-shipper, and profit by $2.

Once you've got your products picked out and a plan in place for shipping the items, it's time to sell. If you already are familiar with eBay and have an account, great! If not, you will have to take a few minutes to set one up. Once you're ready to log-in the process is as easy as 1-2-3:

1. Create/open up an account
2. Follow the format and instruction eBay gives you for selling an item, and
3. Post your items

See! Simple. Make sure to give a detailed/precise description of the product you're selling as well as a clear picture so buyers know what to expect. By picking the right items and selling them for reasonable prices, you should see the money start to come in. Some of you might be contented with this stream of income simple selling provides, but let me go ahead and tempt you with something a little sweeter... your very own eBay store.

That's right; you can open your own e-Bay Store! Having an e-Bay store allows you to show all of your product listings in one location so that potential buyers can see everything you're selling all at once. You'll also be given a unique web address for customers to find you. This unique address can be great for embedding in a blog if you have one, or sharing store info and specials on different social media sites. You even have the opportunity to design your eBay store to your liking. Having an e-Bay store will increase the chances of profitable business and user acclaim.

Q & A

So what should I sell? Well, that's entirely up to you, although it's best to have some sort of niche market you feel confident in catering too. This doesn't mean you need to sell one specific item, but if you stick to one category in general (like dog toys and accessories, for example) you'll quickly develop a reputation for yourself as one of the go to eBay sellers for those types of products. You'll also be able to choose from a wide variety of items from your specialty, so you'll be able to instantly promote items you can get a good deal on.

Where do I find the items I want to sell? It's easy! Just think of some of the items you would be interested in selling and do some preliminary searches for information about said items on the internet (try using keyword searches like "bulk", "wholesale", and "resale" to help hone your search results). When you're searching, you'll want to be on the lookout for a few things. First, look for a company that makes the item. This way you can check if the company has several other products in your category, which will give you the option to reduce the number of different companies you'll have to work with. Next, check and see if the company offers drop shipping. While most drop shippers are essentially middlemen, some businesses actually offer drop shipping or work with a master distributor. If the business doesn't do drop shipping you'll have to either find a drop shipper who does ship that item, or order stock directly from the company with plans to store it at a place of your designation and ship the items to customers yourself.

How do I open an eBay store? To open an e-Bay store you must meet some standard requirements:

- ❖ Have an eBay seller's account with a credit card placed on

file,
- ❖ Have a verified premiere Pay Pal account, and
- ❖ Have a seller performance rating of standard or higher.

All of these are relatively easy to obtain. You'll have the seller account just by signing up for eBay and adding a credit card to your file only takes minutes. Getting a verified Pay pal account is as easy, and if you treat your buyer's right, your seller status will increase after every sale.

A Quick Review…

When getting ready to set shop in the online bazaar that is eBay, you'll want to make sure you:

- ❖ Have an eBay account in good standing

- ❖ Determine product(s) you wish to sell and the best way to ship them (choices might vary depending on business plan).

- ❖ If opening an eBay store, focus on high customer satisfaction and feedback

I've outlined in brief the steps that lay before you on your path to becoming an eBay retailer, but it will still be up to you to make sure your brand and/or store is marketed effectively and efficiently.

Chapter 3 – Blogging

Anyone who has browsed the web knows what a blog is. It seems everyone is using one. From fortune 500 companies to your own friends and family members.

Blogs have a myriad of uses. Individuals may use them to journal personal thoughts. Online stores to show new products. Business' to keep their customers up to date.

And of course the idea we're most interested in – blogs can be used to make money.

To make money, the blog is used much like a static website. The owner puts effort into creating great content to attract visitors. Money is mainly made from advertising, product sales and affiliate revenue.

If the blog attracts a lot of visitors (traffic) per month, advertisers will be happy to pay a monthly rate to place their ads. Alternatively, the blog owner may have its own product to sell, or place his own ads to make commission from other people's products.

Blog owners can even be paid when people simply click an ad. An example is the commonly used Google Ad Sense ads. You have probably seen these ad blocks many times on different sites. If you have ever clicked an ad, the blog or site owner instantly earned a payment.

Successful blogs attract a huge amount of traffic. Hundreds of thousands of people may visit in a single month. There is a lot of revenue to be made.

To make a full time living, there are a couple of routes to take.

The first is to develop a blog to attract massive traffic like the above example. The second is to create multiple *niche* blogs. Each one adding an extra revenue stream. Don't underestimate this though, there is a lot of work to be done whichever way you choose.

How to Create a Profitable Blog

Creating any blog or website needs to begin with research. There will be little point in choosing any old subject and hoping for the best. This is a sure way to failure.

Your passions versus "What makes money"

A lot of authors say that it is good to base a blog on something you are passionate about. Then there is the other side of the coin, which says of course that the subject matter needs to be something that will make you money.

This can make things difficult. The reason why the subject you choose needs to fit your passions and interests, is because blogging is a long-term project. It will keep on paying you, but you need to keep feeding it quality content.

After a while, things can get difficult when it comes to writing decent content. The novelty of the initial pleasure of writing about something you love may have worn off, or you may have run out of ideas. If the subject is about something you are not particularly interested in, it's extremely easy to simply give up and leave it as a lost cause.

Being passionate about the subject means that you will always enjoy writing about it, and your passion will show through in your writing. This goes towards keeping visitors happy and engaged in the content.

So you have to strike a balance. The best way to begin this is to list down all of your interests, passions and hobbies. If you can't think of anything, ask yourself this question: "If I had all the free time and money I needed, what would I spend my time doing?" And no, watching TV and eating donuts is not a good blog subject. What do you love to talk about? What are your hobbies? What kind of books do you own?

Now you have a list of possible blog ideas, you need to do some initial research to see if the things you are passionate about can be profitable. Find out if there is enough interest in the chosen subject, and if there are a lot of buyers in the niche.

Step #1 – How to Research

Magazines. One simple way to analyze demand for a niche is to see if there is a magazine for it. If a publishing company is willing to invest in creating a magazine for the subject, then there must be an audience. An audience willing to spend money on related information.

Books. Another is to check out if there are any related books on the Amazon bestseller list. If a book on the subject is selling well, then that niche is very much in demand.

Keyword tools. There are software applications and online tools that tell you how many searches a certain keyword phrase gets per month on the major search engines. The best one is Google's free keyword tool. Just Google "keyword tool", and it will come straight up.

Type in a keyword or phrase, and the tool will give you a bunch of related phrases, and tell you how many times they are being searched. Some phrases have thousands of searches a day, and some maybe 1 or 2. There is little point in proceeding if the search volume is very low, because a lot of your traffic will be from search engines.

Step #2 – Choose a Name

This will depend entirely on your niche or subject matter. If your blog is about one single type of item, then the name should contain the researched keyword phrase in it. Or, if the blog is intended as a hub concentrating on a variety of subjects in one area, then the name should reflect this.

As an example, if the blog is very specifically about ink-jet cartridges, then you'll want a name that contains this, like "bestinkjetcartridges" as an example.

The blog name could be one of the keyword phrases you researched earlier. This is good because it may rank better in the search results. And, if there was a big search volume, this can provide a lot of traffic.

It's also a good idea to register a domain name. This will make the blog more professional, and also help with search engine rankings.

Step #3 – Create Your Blog

It can be very easy to create a blog on a free site like Blogger.com or WordPress.com. A professional looking blog can be up and running in minutes.

However, this is not the best long-term solution. The trouble is, although the service is free, and they are incredibly easy to use – the blog will never truly belong to you. It will always be at the whim and mercy of the owner company. The above mentioned sites are very well known for simply deleting blogs they dislike, or freezing the account on blogs they believe are "spammy", even if the author made a simple mistake.

This can by a heart-wrenching moment when you realize that hundreds or hours of written work and promotion vanish without warning – along with any revenue.

That is why it's better to host the blog on a server that you have full control of. This may sound a little difficult and expensive, but that's not the case. Modern shared hosting can cost as little as $4 a month.

Most hosting companies will provide an option where you simply click the mouse a couple of times and a new blog will be created.

Step #4 – Create Your Content

After deciding on your niche, it's important to figure out what kind of content your target audience enjoys. A good way to research this is to visit already popular blogs, see what kind of content they regularly serve.

To continue generating quality content that attracts repeat visitors, get yourself well immersed in the niche. Visit forums, message boards and other online hangouts. Find out what your crowd is hungry for. Try Q & A sites like Yahoo Answers to see what questions are being asked.

If you can do the research and provide the answers, visitors will flock to your blog, you will be seen somewhat as an authority, and word of mouth will eventually snowball your visitor numbers.

Step #5 – Driving Traffic

Content is one thing. Getting people to see that content is another. Unfortunately, it's not a case of "if you build it, they will come". If no one knows about it, no one will visit. Your efforts will be wasted.

You will need to spend as much time, or more so on driving traffic to your blog. Or perhaps, if you have the capital, outsource it. Either way, it must be done.

Traffic will come automatically once the blog is more established. If visitors love the content, they will be able to sign up to your RSS feed. Then every time you add a new post, they will be updated.

Here are the main ways to drive traffic:

Blog commenting. This, in my opinion, is one of the best ways to bring initial traffic to any new blog. The visitors are targeted, and the traffic can be continuous. Not only that, but do it right, and you can have a mountain of traffic the day you write your post.

This simply involves interacting and commenting on other blogs in your niche. For each comment, you are allowed to link back to your own website or blog. Make sure your comments are relevant to the post you are commenting on. Be as helpful as possible to ensure the blog owner approves your comment. After a short while, you will start to become recognized by other blog readers.

The more knowledge you share, the more recognized your name will become. This leads to people more likely to click your link, resulting in long term visitors. Depending on the popularity of the other blog post, this can provide traffic for many months.

Guest posting. Just as allowing other authors to create content for your blog, it can also be hugely beneficial to follow the same strategy. Writing high quality articles and requesting to use them as guest posts can land you a lot of traffic. This is especially effective if you manage to get permission to write for a very popular blog. It would almost be like temporarily borrowing their traffic.

Search engine optimization (SEO). Getting your pages high up in the search results from search engines like Google can provide a mountain of traffic. To do this, individual blog posts will need to be optimized for certain keyword phrases, allowing search engines to pick up on this and display your site in the search results.

The keyword phrase needs to be used in the post title, content, and tags. One way of boosting search rankings is for the post to be linked to from other sites on the internet. The higher quality sites linking to your post will really boost the rankings. One of the best ways to do this is to write guest posts and link back in your bio.

Your audience. If you encourage your readers to sign up to your mailing list, or better still, your rss feed, then each time you make a post, they will be notified. Previous happy visitors are more than willing to revisit to check out your new post. And the bigger the list, the more traffic.

Social bookmarking. Adding the ability for your visitors to bookmark your site can really create a viral effect. Certain plugins for your blog can easily allow you to do this. At a click of a button, the visitor will be able to share your content with every friend on their social profile.

Paid traffic. You can pay for traffic, but this is usually only used to gain more subscribers, or when you know the advertising is paying off.

Social media. Sites like You Tube, Digg, Stumbleupon and Facebook are traffic powerhouses. Interacting with fans, and consistently submitting quality content to these social hubs will provide unending traffic.

Q & A

What happens if I run out of ideas for content? This is a common pitfall in creating a profitable blog. The creator eventually runs out of ideas, or suffers burnout from continuous writing. The answer is to use other sources than your own typing hands.

If you keep a keen ear to what's going on in your niche, you'll never run out of ideas for blog posts. Visit forums, user groups, and social sites like Technorati and Digg to keep up to date with the latest goings on and opinions. Create posts revealing your opinion on the most current and pressing issues.

Also remember, it doesn't have to be you that posts. Some of the most popular blogs on the internet utilize guest posting and interviews from other authors. You'll easily find willing participants once you begin to generate long term, regular traffic.

Ideas for blog posts include product or book reviews, responding to another blog, reader questions, and a list of resources. And if you can't do this, try sites like EzineArticles.com for pre-written articles. You are allowed to copy any article in full as long as you keep the resource box in tact.

How do I make money? There are many ways to make money with a blog, providing you have consistent traffic.

Google Ad Sense, Yahoo Content Network, Bing and others allow you to put ad blocks on your site. Each time they are clicked, you get paid.

Affiliate revenue. Advertise affiliate products like eBooks (Click Bank, RapBank), or physical products (Amazon.com). Each time a visitor buys, you will get commission.

Advertisements. If your blog has consistent traffic. Let your readers know that they can advertise banners or links for a fixed monthly fee.

CPA (call per action). Some networks will pay you each time a visitor fills out their email address or signs up for a trail from their ad.

CPM. Other networks will let you put an ad on your site that pays per impression. Every 1000 displays of the ad will pay you a certain amount.

A Quick Review...

When using blogging as an online income, you'll want to make sure you:

- ❖ Thoroughly research to determine a profitable "niche". One that not only has an active and interested crowd, but that you can monetize in the future.
- ❖ Be consistent with your blogging efforts, and be patient enough for the blog to become established.

If you are willing to put in the long-term effort to establish a blog, it can be a very profitable venture. Some successful blog owners make tens of thousand of dollars on a monthly basis.

Your day-to-day activities will revolve around creating great content, interacting with visitors, and driving traffic.

Chapter 4 – Flipping Websites

The term "flipping" derives from the purchase and sale of real estate. The idea being that the investor acquires a property, then flips (resells) it for profit, sometimes within a short period of time.

The same idea applies to website flipping. The buyer purchases what is sometimes known as "virtual real estate", makes fixes or changes to make the site more desirable, then resells for profit.

Single websites regularly sell on average for 6-8 times its monthly income. Savvy buyers with a knack for marketing can increase their sale profits substantially by increasing the monthly income of the site.

As an example, a site could be for sale that has a small income of $50 a month. This could be purchased for up to $400. A buyer may see potential in the site, understanding how to maximize and scale the existing advertising efforts. Doing this alone would improve the income, without altering the current site structure. After these efforts, the website starts making $150 a month on a consistent basis.

If the owner can show proof of these consistent earnings, the site can then be sold for around $1200, earning over 2 ½ times the initial investment (this can be done within a few months). And this is at the low end of the scale. In popular online marketplaces, websites regularly sell for tens of thousands of dollars.

Creating Sites From Scratch

Another angle to website flipping is site creation. This is the safer, lower risk way to trade, because it can be done with very little investment. New sites can be created and sold at the marketplace as "startup sites", meaning it's a new site, with no income or visitors.

Startup sites will not sell as well as a website with established traffic and/or income. However, building up a buyers list from previous customers can be a very good tactic to continue to easily sell new sites.

Who Can Do Site Flipping?

Flipping can be one of the easiest and quickest way to make an income on the internet, but it is best suited to those who have capital to start with. The beginner will also need to spend some time getting up to speed with regards to what sells easiest, and where to buy. Without this knowledge, it can be easy to make investments that could possibly lose you money.

How to Begin Flipping

For beginners, the safest way to start a flipping career is to create websites and make them profitable. This will involve building up organic traffic levels, monetizing the site properly, and keeping detailed analytics of monthly income and traffic.

A shortcut here is to purchase a low cost, pre-made startup site and work from there. This will enable you to get your feet wet with your first purchase without risking a large cash outlay.

Tips

Find out what is selling. The bigger online marketplaces like

Flippa.com allow you to inspect older auctions. You can filter the results to see what has been selling well this month, or even the day before.

Use this knowledge to build similar, even replica sites to resell later on. This information will safeguard any efforts from going to waste, and sites not selling.

Offer big bonuses. Some of the best sellers (especially startup websites) offer nice bonuses to entice buyers. Good ideas for bonuses include free hosting, free site transfer, help with marketing the buyer's new site and so on.

Diligence. Thoroughly research any site you intend on buying. Unfortunately there are more than a few hucksters in the "flipping" world. Con men can make a quick buck by faking statistics, faking site ownership, or lying about the income. Although there are many safeguards to prevent this, it still happens.

Use your due diligence to investigate all claims made about a site for sale before bidding.

It's not only online marketplaces that sell websites. Think outside of the box and try contacting site owners to see if they want to sell. There are a staggering amount of sites built that the owner is no longer interested in. If you see a site that looks somewhat dilapidated and not cared for, make the owner a decent offer (if you see profit potential).

A Quick Review

Flipping websites is an enjoyable way to make an income online. In many ways it is quicker and easier than other, perhaps longer-term paths to make money online. However, as with anything, there are pitfalls.

Without a decent ground knowledge of internet marketing and website building, or little insight into into valuing websites, it can become easy invest in the wrong kind of virtual real estate, without being recuperating the initial outlay.

The best way to start for newcomers is to create startup websites to sell. These can be sold by themselves, or built upon to make them profitable enough to sell for profit. Doing this in the initial stages will build up your knowledge enough to be able to invest wisely in undervalued websites in order to "flip" for quick profits.

Resources

http://www.Flippa.com
The largest, and most frequently used online marketplace (the eBay of site flipping).

http://forums.digitalpoint.com
http://BuySellWebsite.com

Further reading:
http://www.FlipWebSites.com/
http://ZacJohnson.com/flip-this-web-site-flippa-and-site-flipping-guide/

Chapter 5 – Amazon Affiliate Marketing

What if, a multinational company, who spent millions of dollars perfecting their sales process, made a proposition to you. They say, on simple terms, that they would gladly pay you every time you refer a customer to their website.

In fact, it gets even better. They say – all you have to do is encourage visitors to click on a unique link or product image assigned to you. Then, if this particular person purchased *anything* from the store (that has millions of product lines) within 24 hours, they will pay you a certain percentage of the sale.

Does that sound like a deal?

Well, I'm here to tell you it's not only possible, but by signing up today, you can make money quickly.

It's true. Amazon has what is known as an affiliate program. This allows people to easily sign up as a partner. Through their own advertising methods, the job of the affiliate is to simply direct visitors to Amazon by encouraging them to click a unique "affiliate link".

When this link is clicked, Amazon will install what is known as a cookie in the users web browser. This unique cookie will last for 24 hours, and tells Amazon that *you* personally referred that visitor. Whatever the visitor purchases from Amazon within those 24 hours will be credited to you. However much the customer chooses to spend, a percentage will be paid to you.

At the end of each month, Amazon will wire any commissions straight to your bank account.

The benefit of Affiliate marketing (especially with Amazon) is that you don't have to put any effort into trying to convert visitors into buyers. Your simply have to refer traffic to Amazon.com through your affiliate link.

There are many ways this can be achieved. Probably the best, and most common way is to create a website on a certain subject, then recommend Amazon items and link to them, or display product images that visitors can click. The link will take them straight to Amazon.com.

Amazon even has an app that can create a web store for you, with each item embedded with your affiliate details. This is like having your own online shop, without any of the hassles e-commerce.

How to Refer Visitors

The ways to promote are endless. For example, you can put your Amazon link in email messages, Facebook pages, social sites, articles, and text messages. In a later chapter of this guide, there is a whole list of techniques to help you drive traffic.

And the real beauty is the endless niche areas you can promote. Whatever your passion or hobby, or niche you choose, there will be Amazon products that you can advertise. And, even if they don't buy that particular item, you will be credited for anything else they buy. It couldn't be more perfect for the affiliate.

Tips:

Higher priced items = higher commissions. If you're going to concentrate on a certain niche, why not go for a niche that sells higher priced items? After all, an interested buyer is an interested buyer. If you're only making a 4-15% of each sale, it stands to reason that you will make a lot more money on higher priced items.

Pre-sell your customers. Not all traffic is equal. People who are in a buying frame of mind are better than those who are simply window-shopping. Unlike other affiliate programs, Amazon cookies expire after 24 hours. That means if they come back to Amazon tomorrow, you won't get your commission.

Therefore, it is a massive advantage if you can pre-sell each visitor. Show them why they should want to purchase a particular item. The best way to do this is from favorable product reviews, or personal recommendations. Many times, an authentic review or recommendation, with a simple written link can provide much more sales than a product image or banner.

This script will build you a store that acts much like a normal e-commerce site. As the visitor browses the site, they can add items to their basket. The clever thing is that the items are also being remotely added to their Amazon.com basket.

Whenever the buyer decides to go to the Amazon checkout – even up to 90 days later, you will still get your commission.

A Quick Review

Becoming an Amazon affiliate is, in some ways, a marketers dream. Being such a massively successful online vendor, they have refined the sales process almost to perfection. Being so recognizable means visitors are way more likely to purchase. Most internet users frequently purchase from Amazon. They trust the site, and have no fears of making a purchase.

However, this is not a get rich quick business. The small downside to working with Amazon is the percentage of each sale is very low, in comparison to other affiliate programs. This can be offset by sending more traffic and/or creating multiple sites with affiliate advertising.

Another benefit is that the more consistent your revenue becomes, the more Amazon will reward you by offering bonus incentives and higher commissions.

Partnering with Amazon will offer a viable, long term relationship that could easily provide a full time commission if you are willing to be persistent.

Resources

Amazon.com affiliate program:
https://affiliate-program.amazon.com
https://affiliate-program.amazon.co.uk

Chapter 6 – Article Writing

If you are a keen writer, then you have struck gold when it comes to making money online.

In fact, I'd go so far to say that, even if your writing is average at best, you can still carve a living online. Your services will be very much in demand.

If you have a good grasp on writing basics, understand how to do basic research on a subject (know how to Google?), and can follow certain techniques of writing, you can begin straight away.

How to Earn Money Writing

There are actually more than a few ways to earn an income from writing. The most obvious one would be freelancing or ghost writing. This is where someone will pay you to write for them.

Another way would be to write articles that contain your affiliate links and submit them to article directories, or create eBooks and short guides to give away. You can write product reviews the same way.

There are even sites that will allow you to submit *any* content of your choosing. When approved, your writing will be published on their website. Each page of the site contains advertising. These companies pay you some of their advertising income, depending on the popularity of your article. The more eyeballs you get to your content, the more you get paid.

And it doesn't stop there. Other opportunities involve being paid to write blog posts, comment on other blogs, answer questions, or even post in forums.

Freelancing

The fastest route to getting paid as a writer is to bid on projects as a freelancer. To do this, you simply need to sign up with one of the freelance giants like Elance.com, Freelancer.com, or ODesk.com. You could do this right now if you wanted to.

Even if you're not established, you can bid on jobs. Everyone needs to start somewhere. Perhaps bid low to begin with, until you have some feedback under your belt. Although the project owners don't know you, they will usually ask for a quick sample to know if you are good enough for the job. Bid on multiple projects each day. You are bound to win one eventually.

And don't worry, there are a huge amount of jobs available, every day of the week. People are constantly submitting new projects. You will have a choice of thousands of different projects that require offers at any one time.

Could you write 10 articles of 500 words each about baby strollers? Perhaps write a press release about an owners new product? What about a simple 200 word review, or a 300 word blog post? The opportunities are endless.

Food for Thought

Specializing in a certain type of writing can really pay off. If you become well known as delivering top results as a sales letter, article, ebook or email writer, you can charge higher fees.

For example, copywriters in top demand charge $15,000 to $25,000 (or more) for a single sales letter!

Q & A

How can I compete? When you first start bidding on freelance sites, you will notice that people frequently outbid you, meaning they will offer to work for extremely cheap. Don't worry about this. It is up to the project owner who they choose. They will know that the low bidders usually supply inferior quality work. The low bidders are from foreign countries, and do not fully understand the English language.

Where can I find writing jobs? As mentioned, the best place to start is freelance sites like Freelancer.com, Elance.com, or Odesk. You can also place an ad for your writing service in marketing forums, like WarriorForum.com.

Other job sites also employ writers and allow them to work from home. A full list of resources is available at the end of the chapter.

Quick Review

Good writing is an excellent skill to possess, and can make you a lot of money online. If you think about it, almost everything you view online involves text. Quality content is in great demand with web developers and marketers.

Freelancing is a good place to start, but remember this is simply trading time for money, much like a job.

Resources

Freelance sites:
http://www.Freelancer.com
http://www.ODesk.com

http://www.Elance.com
http://www.Guru.com

Other sites to find writing jobs:
http://CraigsList.com
http://Workaholics4Hire.com
http://Online-Writing-Jobs.com

Income from submitting content:
http://www.Helium.com
http://www.AssociatedContent.com
http://www.Triond.com

Article directories (for affiliate sales):
http://www.EzineArticles.com
http://www.GoArticles.com
http://www.ArticlesBase.com

Chapter 7 – Information Products

If you can write small reports, you can make a living online.

Imagine writing an ebook around 15-30 pages long, and selling it for $27. Not only that, but once published to the web, it can be sold over and over again, and digitally delivered to each customer without any further effort from you.

You might think we already discussed this in the previous chapter, but this is different. Instead of being paid to write, you create your own report and sell copies of it, much like traditional book publishing.

These online books are called eBooks, or information products. It allows the buyer to download the ebook instantly, ready to read on their device or to print out.

Traditionally, these reports are sold by creating a website and sales page, including a payment process which automatically delivers the report after payment.

The business has expanded now with the advent of the Amazon Kindle store, allowing anyone to instantly publish their content to sell.

The best way to make an income from ebook sales is to provide solutions to problems that people may be having. People are more than willing to purchase information that will teach them how to remedy a problem, remove pain, or improve their lives.

If you are the publisher of such information, you stand to profit.

The real money is made from what is known as the "back end". That is, once a customer buys the report, they will sign up to an email list. This provides opportunity to market further information products to a targeted list of previous buyers.

What to Write About

It is a good idea to read the section called *"Your passions versus what makes money"* in the blogging chapter. The same rules apply. It may be easier to write something you are passionate about, but at the same time, it must be something people are willing to pay for.

Here is a short list of hot topics to write about:

- Making Money
- Self help/personal development
- Weight loss
- Dating
- Every day problems
- Hobbies
- Recipes
- Tutorials

Writing the Ebook

Writing the ebook is not half as hard as it sounds. There are many ways to create content for an information product once you have chosen a niche. You are only there to provide the answers to problems that people are desperate to solve. The format of the content can be in written word, video, or even an audio interview.

An easy way to get clues on chapter headings is to look at what already exists. Go to Amazon and click on "Look Inside" image on a few different books. The content pages will provide many different ideas.

Also, look to Q & A sites and forums in the niche to see what people are asking. They are asking these questions because they cannot find a satisfactory answer from simply browsing the web.

Once the ebook is written, you'll need to create a sales page explaining the benefits of purchasing. Show the target audience that you feel for them, you've maybe been in their place, and you can provide some of the answers they are looking for.

If there is competition, show the potential customer that you provide a unique approach. Show why it is more advantageous to buy your product than anyone else's. Why they should buy from YOU.

This need not be too complicated, either. A simple web page will usually suffice, with a buy button. The delivery of the ebook can be automated by creating a Pay Pal button that redirects to the download page after payment.

Of course, a sales page won't be necessary if you are submitting your ebook to Amazon in Kindle format.

Outsourcing

In the last chapter we discussed using freelance sites to bid on projects. Turn this around, and *you* become the employer. You now know there are thousands of writers ready and willing to work for you. The entire product can be completely outsourced if you so desire.

Selling the Ebook

If you are creating a Kindle ebook, selling is as simple as uploading to the right category, and entering the right keywords so buyers will find it. Creating a sales page is not necessary, but may help you sell more copies if you redirect potential buyers to the Kindle store.

If you are selling the ebook in the traditional way, selling more all comes down to driving traffic to the sales page.

More sales can be made by offering an affiliate program. You will pay affiliates a certain amount per sale. Adding your site to Click Bank will set this up for you instantly. If you show your sales page has a good conversion rate (percentage of visitors that purchase), affiliates will be very willing to promote for you.

Food for Thought

Companies like CreateSpace and Lightning Source can publish your ebook in paperback format. By agreeing to let them take a certain percentage per sale, your ebook will be available on Amazon.com as a physical book!

This is not like traditional publishing. You won't need to order thousands of copies in advance. The book will literally be printed each time a customer orders a copy.

Tips:

You don't have to *sell* the ebook to make money. You can create something known as a "viral report". The ebook is free, but contains affiliate links. Each time someone orders something based on your recommendation, you will be paid.

More will be distributed, because the ebook is free. You could allow each customer to distribute as many copies as they would like. Providing it is a high quality report, they will be more than happy to oblige.

Build your list. The bigger your email list, the more copies you can sell of your ebook. Building a list before releasing the new ebook will generate many more sales.

Add more members to your list by asking people to opt in to your auto-responder to get something for free.

Quick Review

Writing eBooks can be very profitable. You won't be able to make money on day one like other methods in this guide, but if you are prepared to work at it, the long-term profits can be amazing.

There is a man named John Reese who is well known among internet marketers. At the time John Reese sold information products as discussed in this chapter.

He is very well known, because, back in 2004 he broke all known records for selling online. On the day he launched his new info product, he made sales in excess of $1,000,000 (within 18 hours of the launch). This was a long time ago, and, from what I've been told, the record has been broken many times since.

This can show you the vast potential of selling information. No, you probably won't make a million, but this is just for illustration purposes. It may be hard to believe that such success is available, but it *is* possible.

Chapter 8 – Forex Trading

Forex stands for foreign exchange. You have more than likely used the foreign exchange before on a small scale, perhaps changing US Dollars for another foreign currency while on holiday.

Money is made on the foreign exchange by trading one currency against another. If the currency you have invested in increases in value, you have made a profit.

Using the same example, let's say you didn't spend any of the money on vacation, returning home with the same amount. If the foreign currency had increased in value, when it comes to trading back into dollars, you would have made money.

Example

Let's say you went to Switzerland. You exchanged 500 dollars for the equivalent in Swiss franc.

The currency code for Swiss franc is CHF. The exchange rate at that time was:

1.00 USD = 0.914000 CHF

So 500 dollars gets you 456.55 Swiss franc.

After an enjoyable two-week vacation, you return home, and still have 456.55 franc (maybe you only used credit card while over there).

Obviously, you would want to change the franc back into dollars. However, the exchange rate is now:

1.00 USD = 0.893110

Or, in reverse,

1.00 CHF = 1.11968

Now, once you changed the 457 franc back into dollars, you find that you now have over $511.

Not bad for doing nothing. Quite a good (unintentional) investment. You have made money on the foreign exchange, by trading one currency against another.

Imagine doing this multiple times in one day, and the trade within minutes rather than weeks, and you'll have an understanding of how trading on Forex works.

Invest more capital, and make more money ($5000 would come back as $5117).

This is essentially how Forex works, only the time scale is a lot shorter (a trade can be done in minutes), and more then one trade would be made per day. You can trade any time of the day, 5 days a week (exchange is closed on weekends).

Forex trading involves a lot of speculation, and certainly has an element of gambling. You are actually betting that a currency you invest in will stay strong, and will increase in value within a certain period of time.

Major Currencies

There are eight *major* currencies traded in the Forex market.

U.S. Dollar	USD
British Pound	GBP

Canadian Dollar	CAD
Australian Dollar	AUD
Japanese Yen	JPY
Swiss Franc	CHF
New Zealand Dollar	NZY
Euro	EUR

Currencies Pairs

Every trade you make will be in a currency pair. Major currency pairs, or cross currency pairs. A major currency pair always uses the USD. Cross currency is two foreign currencies.

The left side of the pair is the base currency. The right is the "counter" currency.

Major currency pairs examples: GBP/USD, USD/CAD, AUD/USD

Cross currency pairs examples: EUR/GBP, CAD/JPY, NZD/CHF

U.S. Dollars accounts for over 80% of all Forex transactions, so most of your trades will be with major currency pairs.

The currency rates are volatile and constantly changing. Using an online trading account, it is possible to buy any amount of currency, and trade for a profit <u>within minutes</u>. Trading on the foreign exchange can be very exciting, but of course there is also risk involved.

You are going to need capital to invest here. A certain amount needs to be kept in your trading account (which can be withdrawn any time). The more the better. If you are onto a sure winner, you'll probably want to invest a larger amount to increase profits.

Those who can make bigger (or smarter) trades, will make more money. The sky is the limit.

Forex trading involves analyzing trends. Once you spot a trend you believe will keep climbing, it is time to invest in that currency. You can then ride the trend until it looks to be reversing, then sell at the new, higher rate.

Each price increment of a currency is called a "pip", meaning percentage in point. For speedy trading, you can literally invest in a certain currency, watch it rise a few pips, then sell at profit. This can be done within minutes.

Speculation

Speculation is the main part of Forex trading. In order to speculate correctly, you will need to become adept at analyzing the market. There are different types of analysis you will need to learn: technical, fundamental and sentiment analysis.

Technical analysis is to study current and historical price movement. It requires looking at chart data for patterns or trends that have formed in the past, and using that as evidence that the price movement has a high probability of repeating itself.

Fundamental analysis means to look at the market, and how it may be influenced by outside events. It requires staying on top of current social and economic events that may effect the economic status of the trading country. If the countries economic future looks good, the currency will also gain strength.

Sentiment analysis is a way of gauging what people are thinking or feeling about the market. Although often overlooked, market sentiment can be critical to your success. Consumer confidence can be very much effected by data obtained from fundamental analysis.

One of the best trading networks, named eToro actually shows a kind of ticker at the top of the screen. Once you log in, you can sit there and watch which currencies are climbing, allowing you to invest instantly. Looking at the individual trend chart more closely will allow you to analyze what the trend is doing. If it looks to be still climbing, you might decide to invest. This visual information display makes trading easy for beginners – even those with little knowledge.

There are different time lines to study in Forex. Analysis charts may show updates every minute, 10 minutes, and hourly for example. Choosing which one to concentrate on will depend on the personality of the trader.

Why Forex?

The positive side to Forex trading is the fact that you don't need to be a millionaire to get started. Some will recommend that you have around $10,000 to play with in order to be serious trader. However, you can begin trading for as little as $25 (sometimes even less), depending on what trading account you sign up with. In fact, certain accounts like learnforexpro.com even give you a $5 sign-up bonus so you can begin trading (and hopefully making profit) from day one.

If you are patient enough to build up the capital from somewhat small profits to begin with, you can make a full time living for a *very* small investment. I know of a few people who simply dabble in Forex and make over $100 a day. To some, this may be chump change, but to a beginner, it could be good enough to replace their current income. The great thing about this is that you can make money your very first day, which is rare in any kind of business.

Any profit you make is immediately added to your online account and you can withdraw some or all at any point.

Q&A

How do I begin trading? You will need to open up an online trading account to begin. There are many available. I personally recommend eToro.com. You could begin by using virtual money until you understand how to trade profitably. When you're ready, you will need to transfer funds into the account in order to begin to trade for real.

The trading platform acts as a broker, and allows you to trade instantly. There will be many analytical tools available within the member area, allowing you to go into great detail and understanding of current fluctuations, and recent (or historical) trends of each currency. These details are usually displayed in a visual graph format.

The "market maker" or broker will ask a commission on each trade. The amount will depend on what trading platform, and what commission structure they are using.

From there, your 'job' will consist of analyzing and speculating trends, then buying or selling based on this information.

How do I minimize risk and prevent money loss? With each trade, you will be able to set a "stop loss". You should never trade without effective stops. You have the option of an equity stop, or chart based stop.

For example, you may want a trade to automatically stop before it eats more than 3% into your account balance. Or, if the currency goes down a certain amount of pips.

A Quick Review

Trading on the foreign exchange is suitable for those looking for a reliable, long-term route to making an income online.

Forex can be very rewarding, but you will need to posses an analytical mind, a good grasp of mathematics, and a lot of patience to succeed long term. Remember, with each speculation and trade, you will be making a 'bet' as to what will happen with one particular currency pair. Each potential reward contains an equal amount of risk.

The amount of capital you have available will determine how much money you make. Although, with patience and perseverance, a small initial capital can be grown each month, compounding your income.

You could trade Forex for a full time living, or just in your spare time.

Resources:

http://www.BabyPips.com
One of the best educational sites for beginners.

Http://www.LearnForexPro.com
Forex information, plus $5 sign-up bonus.

http://www.Etoro.com
Recommended online trading platform.

Conclusion

This guide has introduced you 8 excellent techniques to making money online.

The rest is entirely up to you. Maybe try each of the techniques and see how you like working them, or immerse yourself into one of them and run with it until you succeed.

Just be sure to stop yourself falling into the trap so many thousands of people do when trying to carve a career for themselves in the online marketplace. The trap is bailing out when things get tough, and trying something new each time. The cycle then repeats. Unfortunately this happens all to often.

When you work from home, there is no boss breathing down your neck, and no deadlines to work to. Therefore accountability is very low. It will be your choice as to whether you watch TV and browse the web all day, or work as hard as can in order to succeed.

Things can, and usually will be difficult at first. Each technique discussed has its downfalls, and each has a learning curve that you'll need to progress through. For freelancing writing and VA work, you may need to build up a portfolio before people feel they are willing to pay you decent money – it will be tough at first.

Affiliate marketing and blogging can be the same. It takes time to build traffic, to establish yourself, and income will be sparse at first. Forex and website flipping will need bigger capital to begin with, and carry some risk.

It's very important to keep motivated and not give up. Stay away from the shiny things that promise you overnight riches, no matter how convincing the sales page. The only ones getting rich with that deal are those selling the product.

Keep to one course and be patient. Devour information and educate yourself. Join forums and chat groups to see what is working the best. Hire yourself a mentor if you are able.

The ones making the big bucks now are the ones that never gave up when everything *seemed* pointless and too difficult.

You will succeed if you persevere.

"Action is the foundational key to all success"

Pablo Picasso

www.ingramcontent.com/pod-product-compliance
Lightning Source LLC
Chambersburg PA
CBHW071542170526
45166CB00004B/1509